Things My Mother Told Me

Walter P. Froemming

Things My Mother Told Me
Copyright © 2020 by Walter P. Froemming

All rights reserved. No part of this publication may be reproduced, distributed, or transmitted in any form or by any means, including photocopying, recording, or other electronic or mechanical methods, without the prior written permission of the publisher or author, except in the case of brief quotations embodied in critical reviews and certain other noncommercial uses permitted by copyright law.

Although every precaution has been taken to verify the accuracy of the information contained herein, the author and publisher assume no responsibility for any errors or omissions. No liability is assumed for damages that may result from the use of information contained within.

ISBN-13:   Paperback: 978-1-64749-139-0

Printed in the United States of America

GoToPublish LLC
1-888-337-1724
www.gotopublish.com
info@gotopublish.com

I dedicate this book to my beautiful,
loving, Christian mother,
Betty Ann Froemming.

Betty Ann Krueger Froemming

Betty Ann Krueger was born on January 16, 1930. Her parents, August and Ann Krueger, owned the August Krueger Bakery on Green Bay Avenue in Milwaukee, Wisconsin. It was the place to shop at that time. When Betty Ann was 16, her father died of a stroke. Her two older brothers were in World War II. Bob was a clerk and Augie was a pilot.

On August 28, 1948, Betty Ann would marry Arthur Froemming and soon after found out that they would have a baby. They had a honeymoon in Quebec, Canada. They lived above Art's parents, Ella and Walter, on Humboldt Boulevard in Milwaukee.

On May 12, 1949, Betty Ann fell off the back of Art's new road grader and Arthur August Froemming was born six weeks early. They had many dinner parties for friends and relatives. Art bought a piano for Betty Ann for their first anniversary. For Christmas that year, Art bought little Art a Lionel train set which my sister has to this day.

In 1950, Art was going to Marquette University to be a civil engineer while working at his newly formed company AP Paving. In 1952, Art graduated from Marquette University. He bought a house on December 16 on Newhall Street in Whitefish Bay, a suburb of Milwaukee. Gail Ann, my older sister, was born on June 1, 1952. That summer they lived in a log cabin by Walter and Ella's place on Lake Michigan in Cedar Grove, Wisconsin. Art bought Betty Ann a fur stole for their fifth anniversary. They joined the Bay Shore Lutheran Church and little Art started kindergarten. In 1954, Art quit AP Paving at the end of the season. At Thanksgiving, Art and Betty Ann took a trip to Acapulco.

In 1955, it was a very happy year in which they met Sam (Janet) and Jack Rief. On April 19, 1956, Walter Paul Froemming was born. That's me. That Christmas, all their children had the chicken pox. In 1957, I was rushed to the hospital with bronchitis. In 1958, it was a wonderful year with a trip to the Caribbean and lots of great parties at their summer home on Lake Michigan, two doors down from Walter and Ella's place in Cedar Grove, Wisconsin. In 1959, they took another trip to Acapulco. In 1960, they went with another couple of New York. In 1962, they went to Ocho Rios, Jamaica. In 1963, they went to Acapulco with Art's brother Walter and his wife Lucille and the Borth's.

The family moved to Decatur, Illinois in 1964. That Christmas, the entire family drove to Acapulco. In 1966, the family moved to Champagne, Illinois where Art taught at the University of Illinois. In 1967, Walter, Art's dad, died from cancer. In 1968, my brother, Art, graduated from high school and joined the navy. On April 16, 1970, Betty Ann's mother, Ann, died of a heart attack. On August 26, 1972, my sister, Gail Ann, married Don Traub. I was in the wedding.

In September 1972, we bought the True Value Hardware in Belgium, Wisconsin and moved into Grandma Ella's lake home. She took our cottage there. On Tuesday, in the middle of the night, my dad had a brain aneurism. On Thursday, December 13, 1973, at about 5 p.m. my dad died.

In 1975, Art, Betty Ann's oldest son, married Shirley Moore. In the summer of 1976, I had my first manic episode and was hospitalized in the psychiatric ward for three months.

In 1977, my mom sold the hardware store. Mom was the office manager and bookkeeper at Cream City Scale in Menomonee Falls, Wisconsin. Elmer, whom we called Butch, rented a room from mom from 1981 to 1990. Butch was mom's companion. Butch was a former Lutheran pastor who then worked at a hardware store. Butch was in a nursing home in Milwaukee for about seven years.

In the summer of 1985, I had my second manic episode. I was living on campus at Concordia University in Mequon, Wisconsin. I spent seven months in a psych ward and a year in a halfway house in Port Washington.

Butch died in 1998. Mom started dating Jack Rief. They loved being together. Mom had Jack over for dinner every Wednesday. I had my own apartment. Jack died of a heart attack in 2008. Mom retired from Cream City Scale in 1996. She worked part-time as a bookkeeper at Leather Unlimited until she was 81 years old. Leather Unlimited was only five miles away. Betty Ann dated Harry until he died in 2015. Harry was a family man.

On July 31, 2015, I came to live with my mother. Betty Ann has five granddaughters, all married now. She has six great-grandsons and five great-granddaughters.

For Betty Ann's 90th birthday we had a great party at the Five Pillars Restaurant. One hundred and five people attended.

Here are some of the many things my mother told me over the years.

Things My Mother Told Me

1. Do your best and leave the rest to God.

2. Wally, you should make a budget for your money.

3. Nothing ever good happens after 1 a.m.

4. Wally, did you take your medication?

5. Love the Lord with all your heart and stay close to God.

6. You should go to church.

7. Wally, your life has been one big party.

8. Wally, you have to quit smoking.

9. They can't take money from any empty basket.

10. Why when it comes to money can't you be more like Grandma Ella?

11. Wally, don't you put money away for a rainy day?

12. Wally, you have to live within your means.

13. Wally, why are you depressed? You know we all love you.

14. Eat your vegetables.

15. Why did you drink so much? You knew it would make you sick.

16. Wally, I know you don't feel good but you can still go to work.

17. Wally, this apartment better be cleaned by the next time I come over.

18. For God's sake Wally, do your laundry.

19. Wally, you spent too much on Christmas.

20. Wally, don't borrow any more money.

21. Wally, don't complain. You have everything you need.

22. Wally, why don't you have a little Christmas club account and put a little money in every time you get money. I do.

23. Wally, don't spend so much on gifts.

24. Wally, you drink too much. You should cut down.

25. Wally, I don't think you eat right.

26. What does your therapist tell you to do?

27. Wally, you need more exercise.

28. Wally, why don't you relax and stop wiggling.

29. Wally, why can't you do the rest of the yard work. You only worked 20 minutes. Are you that out of shape?

30. Wally, you have a lot of good friends.

31. Wally, all your friends drink.

32. Accomplish at least one thing a day.

33. Wally, you procrastinate.

34. Your sister does a lot for you.

35. This winter is too long.

36. Did you ever think of reading your Bible?

37. Wally, you travel a lot. My grandma never left Wisconsin.

38. Wally, all you want to do is fun things.

39. Take it to the Lord in prayer.

40. Wally, your clothes smell like smoke.

41. We need to laugh more.

42. Wally, is this the way you want to keep your apartment? It's worse than your brother Art's house.

43. Wally, you need a hobby. I garden.

44. Wally don't be so concerned with the way the girl looks. You want to date but concentrate on the inside.

45. Wally, you are using your mental illness as an excuse.

46. Wally, I spoiled you.

47. Wally, how do you think you're going to get a girlfriend if you don't shave and clean up and cut your nails.

48. Wally you have the time to get your daily chores done. It's not like you work fulltime or have kids.

49. Wally, know your limitations.

50. Wally, expectations lead to frustration.

51. Wally, don't live in the past.

52. Wally, we tell you and tell you but you still don't listen. You still do the things you're not supposed to do.

53. Believe in yourself.

54. My brother says I'm lost in the 70's but that's another book.

55. Why don't you have the confidence your brother Art has?

56. Wally, it's great you don't drink anymore.

57. Wally, don't you like to read?

58. Wally, I don't think you get enough sleep.

59. Wally, I know you just drink soda but you don't have to stay out until the bar closes.

60. Don't just think about yourself.

61. Wally, at least you're on time.

62. Wally, did you ever think about cleaning out your car?

63. You can do what you want but you have to pay the consequences. My niece Julie said that but that's another book.

64. Wally, it's not your birthday today.

65. Wally, we told you to stop gambling.

66. It is not what you have but how you use it.

67. Stop your crying or I'll give you something to cry about. My dad said that but that's another book.

68. People in Hell want ice water. Maybe it was my dad who said that too.

69. Your soda would taste better if you put it on ice.

70. Wally, why don't you drink diet soda. You're drinking too much sugar.

71. Wally, you have quite the imagination.

72. Wally, you can play after you get your work done.

73. Wally, you drink too much. More than all of us.

74. Your dad never did that.

75. Well your uncles smoked cigars.

76. Wally, you have a lot of music CD's.

77. Don't you ever watch the news?

78. I'll tell you who to vote for.

79. Wally, I'm proud of you.

80. Wally, you are very generous.

81. Wally, you're a nice guy.

82. I don't see why you don't have a girlfriend. You're a good looking guy.

83. Wally, you don't need to get married.

84. Wally, you don't look your age.

85. Wally, I didn't think you could fix that.

86. Wally, how can you watch the same movie over and over?

87. Do it now. Then it's done.

88. Wally, I am glad you like girls.

89. Wally, you are the only one I know who can sell cats.

90. Wally, you have a lot of girlfriends.

91. You're not a kid anymore.

92. Wally, I'm disappointed in you.

93. Wally, get some sleep.

94. Wally, I didn't know you like deer meat.

95. Don't let your sister see that my brother-in-law Don said that but that's another book.

96. Wally, you're not telling us everything.

97. Wally, what did you do with your refund?

98. Wally, that's not funny.

99. Wally, we're not going to do that for you.

100. Wally, you think too much.

101. Wally, why didn't you do it right the first time?

102. Wally, you got your days and nights mixed up again.

103. Wally, I bet you sabotaged your sleep again.

104. Wally, at least you go to the dentist, not like your brother Art.

105. Wally, no way should you go to Las Vegas.

106. Wally, no more Coke for you today.

107. Wally, your birthday dinner is easy – pizza.

108. Wally, you should eat yogurt. It would help you go to the bathroom.

109. Just think it you had all the money you spend on cigarettes.

110. Wally, you're allergic to money.

111. Wally, if you didn't have to pay back the money you borrowed, you could have money.

112. Wally, you don't care what the weather is like, do you?

113. Wally, you shouldn't hitch hike.

114. Wally, don't you ever make your bed?

115. Wally, you need to brush your teeth.

116. We think you need to comb your hair.

117. Wally, when are you going to grow up?

118. Wally, you should set goals.

119. Wally, you should make a list of the things you need to get done. I do.

120. Some things are best unsaid.

121. You've been friends with Danny a long time.

122. Wally, you're hard on your cars.

123. Wally, running out of gas like you do is hard on your cars.

124. Wally, do you change the oil on your car?

125. Wally, do you have food in the house? I'll give you some.

126. Wally, it's expensive to go out to eat all the time.

127. Wally, why don't you have any money? What do you do with it?

128. You don't have enough money to give it away.

129. Wally, you don't get enough money from the people you drive around.

130. Be thankful for what you have.

131. Wally, you have always gotten everything that you wanted.

132. Wally, is there a bar that you haven't been in?

133. Don't be a procrastinator. Act like Danny.

134. You took another mental health day. I hope you don't lose your job.

135. Wally, did you miss church again?

136. Wally, I don't know why you can't keep a girlfriend.

137. You attract weird people.

138. Wally, I don't know what makes you think you can sing. (Maybe my brother said that.)

139. Wally, your beard makes you look 20 years older.

140. Wally, I don't understand it. You don't worry about anything.

141. Even Wally made it through college. (What does she mean by that?)

142. Wally, I think you're hard of hearing.

143. Wally, remember, you don't have the money Bill Gates does.

144. Wally, ever think of saving money for your old age?

145. Wally, you need to eat fruit.

146. Wally, you should take vitamins.

147. Wally, you should get a flu shot.

148. Wally all that caffeine you drink in Coke is not good for you. Doesn't it keep you up at night?

149. You got pains now – wait until you're my age.

150. Wally, I don't know how you get people to clean your apartment for you.

151. Wally, can't you find something else to do besides go to the tavern?

152. Wally, I think you have a little dog that shits money.

153. Wally, you ever think of doing a little work?

154. Wally, how much money did you waste gambling?

155. Wally, you are a good gift giver.

156. Wally, you don't know how to cook.

157. Wally, you make good spaghetti.

158. Wally, you spend too much time in your recliner.

159. Wally, you're getting new glasses again?

160. Wally, I would be embarrassed.

161. Wally, I didn't think you would eat that all.

162. Wally, your eyes are bigger than your stomach.

163. Wally, do you ever dust?

164. Wally, how much coke do you drink in a day?

165. Wally, how many cigarettes do you smoke in a day?

166. Wally, you always want the most expensive things.

167. Wally, you don't need the best one.

168. Wally, you really like ice cream!

169. Wally, how can you sit around all day?

170. Wally, you're no different than anyone else. (I beg to differ.)

171. Wally, do you really need a cat?

172. I hope I don't get Alzheimer's.

173. Wally, you put burn holes in all of your clothes. That's another reason to quit smoking.

174. Wally, maybe you should have a drink.

175. Wally, if you take a Xanax, you should not drive.

176. I'm glad I'm not in school.

177. Wally, if you don't do it, I'll have to hire someone.

178. Wally, you drank all my coke again.

179. Wally, thank you for taking out the garbage.

180. Wally, how many cars have you had?

181. Wally, you don't need a motorcycle.

182. Wally, don't buy back your dad's motorcycle. Get a new one.

183. Well, Wally, you can try to make me happy. It doesn't take much.

184. Wally, you have champagne taste on a beer budget.

185. Wally, how can you live like that?

186. How do you know they think that?

187. The weatherman doesn't care if he is right.

188. Your brother Art has to be the first to see a new movie.

189. Choose your friends wisely.

190. Keep the faith.

191. Keep writing.

192. Do you drink anything else but Coke? Try water.

193. Wally, you don't drink enough water.

194. I'm taking a Tylenol PM and you're taking two of them.

195. Wally, did you go in the lake at all? Last summer the water was warm.

196. Wally, if you don't have the money, you can't do that.

197. Wally, you have to take better care of yourself.

198. Wally, take pride in yourself.

199. Wally, not everything is black and white.

200. Honesty is the best policy.

201. Don't forget to help others.

202. Wally, you don't show any emotion.

203. Wally, you are over sensitive.

204. ally, you don't know the value of money.

205. It's easier to smile than frown.

206. Wally, couldn't you wear something nicer.

207. Wally, you need a haircut.

208. Waste not, want not.

209. Wally you work part-time. Why don't you volunteer somewhere?

210. Wally, you're good with the elderly and disabled.

211. Wally, you have more patience than I have.

212. Wally, if you went out less it would be more fun when you did go out. Like a treat.

213. I love chocolate.

214. I love gardening.

215. Wally, thank you for the gifts.

216. With all the driving you do, how can you afford the gas?

217. Everyone spends their money differently.

218. If you're not going to do it right, why bother.

219. Beer is better for you than all that soda.

220. Wally, you don't go through your clothes and get rid of some.

221. Where do you get all your clothes?

222. Your sister Gail says not to lend you my ear.

223. Your sister Gail says not to lend you money.

224. Wally, I like the way you decorated your apartment.

225. Wally, it's good that you have life insurance.

226. Wally, go for a walk.

227. Dr. John and Debbie are so very good to you.

228. Wally, I don't see what you see in her.

229. Not another one like Susie.

230. Robin probably won't go again. I don't know why you ask her to go places with you.

231. Wally, you'd better take a shower.

232. Wally, you are good at making crafts.

233. Wally, people like the poems you write for them.

234. I like your Christmas poems.

235. Keep up the good work.

236. Wally, I don't know how you work third shift. I couldn't.

237. Don't they make a schedule for you at work?

238. Wally, it would be good if you had a routine.

239. Third shift work messes up your sleep schedule.

240. I don't think third shift work is good for you.

241. Wally, I don't know how you can lose your phone.

242. How many times have I told you it doesn't help.

243. Wally, cut your toenails.

244. Wally, sometimes you're a dirty old man.

245. Wally, you walk like an old man.

246. Wally, I'm glad you drink Crystal Lite at home and not soda.

247. Wally, you talk in your sleep.

248. Wally, you don't need a vacation. You only work part-time.

249. Why at 57 do you still dress up for Halloween?

250. I hate bowling.

251. Try playing cards with your friends. Reply: I'll play strip Poker.

252. Our family is getting too big.

253. I can't drink like I used to.

254. I can't eat everything I used to.

255. Wally, you may have sleep apnea.

256. Wally, we should fix your grandfather's clock.

257. Wally, you are kind.

258. I can't afford to go to a Packer's game, how can you?

259. Wally, don't be so lazy.

260. Wally, what's your problem?

261. Wally, you don't apply yourself.

262. Wally, I appreciate all your help.

263. Wally, can you shovel the walk?

264. Wally, can you cut the lawn? I don't think your brother Art is going to do it.

265. Wally, we gave you a lot of money already.

266. Wally, you're going to have to buy a car with your own money and pay cash.

267. Wally, another new therapist?

268. I'm glad you always take your medication.

269. Wally, it's a good idea to make a schedule for your chores.

270. Wally, how many times do I have to tell you?

271. Wally, you should shave every day. It's not that hard.

272. Quit playing the lottery. You'll never win.

273. Keep an open mind.

274. Listen to your sister. She is trying to help you.

275. I can't believe you round off the amount in your checkbook. How do you balance your checkbook?

276. When are you going to learn how to handle your money?

277. If you told the truth you wouldn't feel bad.

278. I don't want you to lie anymore. Just face the consequences.

279. If you didn't borrow from people, you wouldn't have to explain your finances.

280. Don't set your goals too high.

281. Pick up the cat food by your cat's feeding bowl.

282. Your roll top desk came in handy for you.

283. You don't and can't help everybody Wally.

284. I can't believe all the different people who stay with you at your apartment.

285. Have you had the gout lately?

286. Wally, this too will pass.

287. Wally, how many shares do you have?

288. Don't forget your brother loves birthdays.

289. Your apartment smells like smoke.

290. You should use deodorant every day.

291. I bet you killed another plant.

292. Is it ever going to stop raining?

293. Life is full of changes. You just have to learn to adjust.

294. You think life is one big party – it's not.

295. I like living in Wisconsin too.

296. Put your hope in the Lord Jesus.

www.ingramcontent.com/pod-product-compliance
Lightning Source LLC
LaVergne TN
LVHW072051060526
838200LV00061B/4710